PLUS OR MINUS

ARITHMETIC PUZZLES

BOOK 1

MACL

2019

PLUS OR MINUS: ARITHMETIC PUZZLES

BOOK 1

ISBN 978-1-989454-02-2

(print book)

MOTHER AND CHILD LEARNING

2019

PLUS OR MINUS Puzzle 1

5	7	2	4	10
6	8	2	2	10
2	1	7	2	8
4	6	2	5	3
9	10	9	3	

Put either a plus (+) or a minus (-) sign beside each number, so the numbers add up to the answers in the right-hand column and in the bottom row. The numbers in the diagonal, the right-hand column and the bottom row all add up to the same number, which is always positive.

All Plus or Minus puzzles are copyright © Laird Stevens 2019.

PLUS OR MINUS Puzzle 2

5	5	3	3	4
5	8	1	2	4
1	7	2	5	3
5	3	2	7	1
6	9	8	3	

Put either a plus (+) or a minus (-) sign beside each number, so the numbers add up to the answers in the right-hand column and in the bottom row. The numbers in the diagonal, the right-hand column and the bottom row all add up to the same number, which is always positive.

PLUS OR MINUS Puzzle 3

3	1	1	3	8
2	5	8	8	9
6	5	7	1	7
2	7	4	1	8
9	8	4	7	

Put either a plus (+) or a minus (-) sign beside each number, so the numbers add up to the answers in the right-hand column and in the bottom row. The numbers in the diagonal, the right-hand column and the bottom row all add up to the same number, which is always positive.

PLUS OR MINUS Puzzle 4

8	5	3	7	9
3	7	2	9	7
7	2	5	8	8
1	4	7	4	2
5	4	3	2	

Put either a plus (+) or a minus (-) sign beside each number, so the numbers add up to the answers in the right-hand column and in the bottom row. The numbers in the diagonal, the right-hand column and the bottom row all add up to the same number, which is always positive.

PLUS OR MINUS Puzzle 5

8	2	4	5	9
5	6	4	4	9
2	2	6	8	6
6	5	1	7	3
9	7	5	6	

Put either a plus (+) or a minus (-) sign beside each number, so the numbers add up to the answers in the right-hand column and in the bottom row. The numbers in the diagonal, the right-hand column and the bottom row all add up to the same number, which is always positive.

All Plus or Minus puzzles are copyright © Laird Stevens 2019.

5

PLUS OR MINUS

5	3	1	6	7
3	6	1	7	5
3	2	5	8	4
3	5	2	4	4
8	4	5	3	

Put either a plus (+) or a minus (-) sign beside each number, so the numbers add up to the answers in the right-hand column and in the bottom row. The numbers in the diagonal, the right-hand column and the bottom row all add up to the same number, which is always positive.

PLUS OR MINUS

6	5	3	1	7
6	1	2	1	8
7	2	6	2	5
3	6	4	8	9
8	4	9	6	

Put either a plus (+) or a minus (-) sign beside each number, so the numbers add up to the answers in the right-hand column and in the bottom row. The numbers in the diagonal, the right-hand column and the bottom row all add up to the same number, which is always positive.

PLUS OR MINUS

6	3	2	2	7
3	2	4	2	7
7	1	3	1	6
1	3	3	6	5
1	3	6	9	

Put either a plus (+) or a minus (-) sign beside each number, so the numbers add up to the answers in the right-hand column and in the bottom row. The numbers in the diagonal, the right-hand column and the bottom row all add up to the same number, which is always positive.

PLUS OR MINUS Puzzle 9

7	9	7	4	5
5	1	6	2	2
1	9	8	9	9
4	9	9	5	9
9	8	4	6	

Put either a plus (+) or a minus (-) sign beside each number, so the numbers add up to the answers in the right-hand column and in the bottom row. The numbers in the diagonal, the right-hand column and the bottom row all add up to the same number, which is always positive.

All Plus or Minus puzzles are copyright © Laird Stevens 2019.

PLUS OR MINUS Puzzle 10

10	5	4	10	9
1	5	6	6	6
9	9	7	5	2
3	1	7	7	2
3	8	10	2	

Put either a plus (+) or a minus (-) sign beside each number, so the numbers add up to the answers in the right-hand column and in the bottom row. The numbers in the diagonal, the right-hand column and the bottom row all add up to the same number, which is always positive.

All Plus or Minus puzzles are copyright © Laird Stevens 2019.

PLUS OR MINUS

5	5	2	4	4
2	6	4	3	9
8	2	3	3	4
9	4	4	8	1
6	9	3	2	

Put either a plus (+) or a minus (-) sign beside each number, so the numbers add up to the answers in the right-hand column and in the bottom row. The numbers in the diagonal, the right-hand column and the bottom row all add up to the same number, which is always positive.

PLUS OR MINUS

7	1	2	6	10
6	9	1	6	8
2	2	2	1	5
3	3	1	2	1
8	9	4	1	

Put either a plus (+) or a minus (-) sign beside each number, so the numbers add up to the answers in the right-hand column and in the bottom row. The numbers in the diagonal, the right-hand column and the bottom row all add up to the same number, which is always positive.

PLUS OR MINUS Puzzle 13

10	5	3	2	10
1	9	8	6	10
3	1	3	3	4
2	6	8	10	10
10	7	10	1	

Put either a plus (+) or a minus (-) sign beside each number, so the numbers add up to the answers in the right-hand column and in the bottom row. The numbers in the diagonal, the right-hand column and the bottom row all add up to the same number, which is always positive.

PLUS OR MINUS Puzzle 14

8	6	4	3	9
3	7	4	5	9
3	5	9	1	6
3	1	2	2	8
5	5	3	3	

Put either a plus (+) or a minus (-) sign beside each number, so the numbers add up to the answers in the right-hand column and in the bottom row. The numbers in the diagonal, the right-hand column and the bottom row all add up to the same number, which is always positive.

All Plus or Minus puzzles are copyright © Laird Stevens 2019.

PLUS OR MINUS Puzzle 15

9	5	2	2	10
7	4	4	1	6
8	3	8	3	10
3	5	3	8	7
7	3	7	4	

Put either a plus (+) or a minus (-) sign beside each number, so the numbers add up to the answers in the right-hand column and in the bottom row. The numbers in the diagonal, the right-hand column and the bottom row all add up to the same number, which is always positive.

All Plus or Minus puzzles are copyright © Laird Stevens 2019.

15

PLUS OR MINUS

3	2	3	1	7
8	4	5	1	8
1	4	3	5	5
3	3	2	1	9
9	9	9	8	

Put either a plus (+) or a minus (-) sign beside each number, so the numbers add up to the answers in the right-hand column and in the bottom row. The numbers in the diagonal, the right-hand column and the bottom row all add up to the same number, which is always positive.

PLUS OR MINUS

7	1	3	2	5
4	8	2	3	9
1	3	7	3	8
5	2	3	4	4
9	2	3	4	

Put either a plus (+) or a minus (-) sign beside each number, so the numbers add up to the answers in the right-hand column and in the bottom row. The numbers in the diagonal, the right-hand column and the bottom row all add up to the same number, which is always positive.

PLUS OR MINUS Puzzle 18

4	5	3	3	5
1	9	3	8	5
1	1	1	4	5
1	6	2	8	5
7	1	7	7	

Put either a plus (+) or a minus (-) sign beside each number, so the numbers add up to the answers in the right-hand column and in the bottom row. The numbers in the diagonal, the right-hand column and the bottom row all add up to the same number, which is always positive.

All Plus or Minus puzzles are copyright © Laird Stevens 2019.

18

PLUS OR MINUS Puzzle 19

4	1	4	2	3
1	6	2	2	5
5	6	8	1	4
3	8	3	7	7
1	9	9	8	

Put either a plus (+) or a minus (-) sign beside each number, so the numbers add up to the answers in the right-hand column and in the bottom row. The numbers in the diagonal, the right-hand column and the bottom row all add up to the same number, which is always positive.

All Plus or Minus puzzles are copyright © Laird Stevens 2019.

PLUS OR MINUS Puzzle 20

9	4	4	1	2
6	3	2	4	5
4	5	2	2	3
4	3	7	1	1
7	5	1	2	

Put either a plus (+) or a minus (-) sign beside each number, so the numbers add up to the answers in the right-hand column and in the bottom row. The numbers in the diagonal, the right-hand column and the bottom row all add up to the same number, which is always positive.

PLUS OR MINUS Puzzle 21

3	6	4	1	4
2	7	2	3	4
1	3	9	1	4
8	2	1	2	5
8	8	8	7	

Put either a plus (+) or a minus (-) sign beside each number, so the numbers add up to the answers in the right-hand column and in the bottom row. The numbers in the diagonal, the right-hand column and the bottom row all add up to the same number, which is always positive.

All Plus or Minus puzzles are copyright © Laird Stevens 2019.

9	1	3	1	10
5	9	4	3	7
1	5	6	1	9
3	4	5	3	1
10	9	10	2	

Put either a plus (+) or a minus (-) sign beside each number, so the numbers add up to the answers in the right-hand column and in the bottom row. The numbers in the diagonal, the right-hand column and the bottom row all add up to the same number, which is always positive.

All Plus or Minus puzzles are copyright © Laird Stevens 2019.

PLUS OR MINUS

8	4	4	9	7
4	7	7	2	8
8	4	9	2	5
7	9	2	7	7
5	6	4	2	

Put either a plus (+) or a minus (-) sign beside each number, so the numbers add up to the answers in the right-hand column and in the bottom row. The numbers in the diagonal, the right-hand column and the bottom row all add up to the same number, which is always positive.

PLUS OR MINUS Puzzle 24

5	3	1	2	5
3	1	2	1	3
4	2	8	3	9
3	4	4	3	2
7	6	7	7	

Put either a plus (+) or a minus (-) sign beside each number, so the numbers add up to the answers in the right-hand column and in the bottom row. The numbers in the diagonal, the right-hand column and the bottom row all add up to the same number, which is always positive.

All Plus or Minus puzzles are copyright © Laird Stevens 2019.

PLUS OR MINUS Puzzle 25

8	1	3	1	9
1	8	6	1	4
1	2	8	1	8
3	4	2	4	1
7	9	7	3	

Put either a plus (+) or a minus (-) sign beside each number, so the numbers add up to the answers in the right-hand column and in the bottom row. The numbers in the diagonal, the right-hand column and the bottom row all add up to the same number, which is always positive.

PLUS OR MINUS Puzzle 26

10	2	5	4	9
1	6	2	8	1
2	7	3	1	7
3	3	4	9	7
8	8	8	2	

Put either a plus (+) or a minus (-) sign beside each number, so the numbers add up to the answers in the right-hand column and in the bottom row. The numbers in the diagonal, the right-hand column and the bottom row all add up to the same number, which is always positive.

All Plus or Minus puzzles are copyright © Laird Stevens 2019.

PLUS OR MINUS

9	1	3	3	10
4	9	3	1	9
4	6	9	1	2
7	4	1	2	8
8	8	8	1	

Put either a plus (+) or a minus (-) sign beside each number, so the numbers add up to the answers in the right-hand column and in the bottom row. The numbers in the diagonal, the right-hand column and the bottom row all add up to the same number, which is always positive.

PLUS OR MINUS Puzzle 28

7	8	4	3	8
2	1	4	2	1
2	2	10	2	8
2	4	5	8	9
9	9	3	9	

Put either a plus (+) or a minus (-) sign beside each number, so the numbers add up to the answers in the right-hand column and in the bottom row. The numbers in the diagonal, the right-hand column and the bottom row all add up to the same number, which is always positive.

All Plus or Minus puzzles are copyright © Laird Stevens 2019.

28

PLUS OR MINUS

8	3	2	2	7
6	1	3	5	7
2	6	7	4	7
3	1	5	9	2
9	9	3	8	

Put either a plus (+) or a minus (-) sign beside each number, so the numbers add up to the answers in the right-hand column and in the bottom row. The numbers in the diagonal, the right-hand column and the bottom row all add up to the same number, which is always positive.

PLUS OR MINUS Puzzle 30

3	3	5	3	4
5	4	4	3	6
3	1	5	8	9
4	2	1	7	8
5	6	7	5	

Put either a plus (+) or a minus (-) sign beside each number, so the numbers add up to the answers in the right-hand column and in the bottom row. The numbers in the diagonal, the right-hand column and the bottom row all add up to the same number, which is always positive.

PLUS OR MINUS Puzzle 31

8	6	1	8	7
4	5	3	1	5
3	4	8	7	8
5	2	6	7	8
6	9	6	7	

Put either a plus (+) or a minus (-) sign beside each number, so the numbers add up to the answers in the right-hand column and in the bottom row. The numbers in the diagonal, the right-hand column and the bottom row all add up to the same number, which is always positive.

All Plus or Minus puzzles are copyright © Laird Stevens 2019.

PLUS OR MINUS Puzzle 32

7	3	2	3	5
3	8	3	7	1
6	1	6	2	1
7	2	3	3	1
5	6	4	1	

Put either a plus (+) or a minus (-) sign beside each number, so the numbers add up to the answers in the right-hand column and in the bottom row. The numbers in the diagonal, the right-hand column and the bottom row all add up to the same number, which is always positive.

PLUS OR MINUS Puzzle 33

6	2	1	1	4
2	7	5	5	5
3	3	4	3	5
4	4	3	4	9
3	4	5	7	

Put either a plus (+) or a minus (-) sign beside each number, so
the numbers add up to the answers in the right-hand column and
in the bottom row. The numbers in the diagonal, the right-hand
column and the bottom row all add up to the same number, which
is always positive.

All Plus or Minus puzzles are copyright © Laird Stevens 2019.

PLUS OR MINUS Puzzle 34

7	2	2	2	1
4	5	3	5	3
5	5	3	2	5
3	3	6	3	3
5	5	2	2	

Put either a plus (+) or a minus (-) sign beside each number, so the numbers add up to the answers in the right-hand column and in the bottom row. The numbers in the diagonal, the right-hand column and the bottom row all add up to the same number, which is always positive.

All Plus or Minus puzzles are copyright © Laird Stevens 2019.

PLUS OR MINUS Puzzle 35

2	2	5	4	5
5	2	3	1	5
2	1	2	5	6
1	2	1	1	3
6	5	3	7	

Put either a plus (+) or a minus (-) sign beside each number, so the numbers add up to the answers in the right-hand column and in the bottom row. The numbers in the diagonal, the right-hand column and the bottom row all add up to the same number, which is always positive.

All Plus or Minus puzzles are copyright © Laird Stevens 2019.

35

PLUS OR MINUS Puzzle 36

4	1	1	4	2
8	4	3	3	2
3	2	4	1	4
3	1	2	4	8
2	2	2	2	

Put either a plus (+) or a minus (-) sign beside each number, so the numbers add up to the answers in the right-hand column and in the bottom row. The numbers in the diagonal, the right-hand column and the bottom row all add up to the same number, which is always positive.

PLUS OR MINUS

2	3	4	3	4
3	7	1	6	3
1	3	8	2	6
8	1	3	5	5
6	6	6	6	

Put either a plus (+) or a minus (-) sign beside each number, so the numbers add up to the answers in the right-hand column and in the bottom row. The numbers in the diagonal, the right-hand column and the bottom row all add up to the same number, which is always positive.

PLUS OR MINUS Puzzle 38

4	8	7	2	17
5	5	5	7	8
3	4	3	4	6
2	7	8	9	4
8	2	1	4	15

Put either a plus (+) or a minus (-) sign beside each number, so the numbers add up to the answers in the right-hand column and in the bottom row. The numbers in the diagonal, the right-hand column and the bottom row all add up to the same number, which is always positive.

All Plus or Minus puzzles are copyright © Laird Stevens 2019.

PLUS OR MINUS

9	7	4	1	7
2	8	6	1	1
4	2	7	3	8
5	2	3	6	4
8	5	8	3	

Put either a plus (+) or a minus (-) sign beside each number, so the numbers add up to the answers in the right-hand column and in the bottom row. The numbers in the diagonal, the right-hand column and the bottom row all add up to the same number, which is always positive.

All Plus or Minus puzzles are copyright © Laird Stevens 2019.

PLUS OR MINUS Puzzle 40

6	2	1	4	5
2	6	1	2	5
1	1	3	1	2
4	2	1	7	8
7	7	4	6	

Put either a plus (+) or a minus (-) sign beside each number, so the numbers add up to the answers in the right-hand column and in the bottom row. The numbers in the diagonal, the right-hand column and the bottom row all add up to the same number, which is always positive.

PLUS OR MINUS Puzzle 41

5	3	4	2	4
5	6	1	4	6
6	2	7	4	7
4	3	2	1	8
8	8	4	3	

Put either a plus (+) or a minus (-) sign beside each number, so the numbers add up to the answers in the right-hand column and in the bottom row. The numbers in the diagonal, the right-hand column and the bottom row all add up to the same number, which is always positive.

PLUS OR MINUS

10	5	7	1	9
4	10	1	4	9
9	3	10	5	9
5	10	8	1	2
10	8	10	1	

Put either a plus (+) or a minus (-) sign beside each number, so the numbers add up to the answers in the right-hand column and in the bottom row. The numbers in the diagonal, the right-hand column and the bottom row all add up to the same number, which is always positive.

All Plus or Minus puzzles are copyright © Laird Stevens 2019.

PLUS OR MINUS Puzzle 43

8	3	6	2	7
3	6	5	1	1
1	4	4	5	2
2	2	6	9	3
4	7	9	1	

Put either a plus (+) or a minus (-) sign beside each number, so the numbers add up to the answers in the right-hand column and in the bottom row. The numbers in the diagonal, the right-hand column and the bottom row all add up to the same number, which is always positive.

PLUS OR MINUS Puzzle 44

8	6	9	1	10
6	9	1	5	1
5	1	2	4	6
2	5	3	9	9
5	7	5	7	

Put either a plus (+) or a minus (-) sign beside each number, so the numbers add up to the answers in the right-hand column and in the bottom row. The numbers in the diagonal, the right-hand column and the bottom row all add up to the same number, which is always positive.

All Plus or Minus puzzles are copyright © Laird Stevens 2019.

44

PLUS OR MINUS Puzzle 45

4	2	4	3	7
4	6	1	7	4
3	4	9	1	1
6	5	2	8	1
5	7	2	1	

Put either a plus (+) or a minus (-) sign beside each number, so the numbers add up to the answers in the right-hand column and in the bottom row. The numbers in the diagonal, the right-hand column and the bottom row all add up to the same number, which is always positive.

PLUS OR MINUS

6	5	4	6	9
7	8	6	2	9
3	3	5	1	4
6	2	7	4	1
8	8	8	1	

Put either a plus (+) or a minus (-) sign beside each number, so the numbers add up to the answers in the right-hand column and in the bottom row. The numbers in the diagonal, the right-hand column and the bottom row all add up to the same number, which is always positive.

PLUS OR MINUS Puzzle 47

7	4	5	3	9
5	8	3	4	4
1	3	2	1	1
5	3	1	9	6
8	6	5	1	

Put either a plus (+) or a minus (-) sign beside each number, so the numbers add up to the answers in the right-hand column and in the bottom row. The numbers in the diagonal, the right-hand column and the bottom row all add up to the same number, which is always positive.

All Plus or Minus puzzles are copyright © Laird Stevens 2019.

47

PLUS OR MINUS Puzzle 48

8	7	1	4	10
3	5	5	2	9
7	4	8	2	9
4	1	4	1	6
8	9	8	3	

Put either a plus (+) or a minus (-) sign beside each number, so the numbers add up to the answers in the right-hand column and in the bottom row. The numbers in the diagonal, the right-hand column and the bottom row all add up to the same number, which is always positive.

All Plus or Minus puzzles are copyright © Laird Stevens 2019.

PLUS OR MINUS

9	4	10	5	8
3	4	3	1	9
2	5	2	3	4
4	3	3	8	6
10	6	2	7	

Put either a plus (+) or a minus (-) sign beside each number, so the numbers add up to the answers in the right-hand column and in the bottom row. The numbers in the diagonal, the right-hand column and the bottom row all add up to the same number, which is always positive.

PLUS OR MINUS Puzzle 50

7	4	6	5	10
5	4	8	9	8
1	7	4	5	5
3	6	1	4	4
8	9	7	5	

Put either a plus (+) or a minus (-) sign beside each number, so the numbers add up to the answers in the right-hand column and in the bottom row. The numbers in the diagonal, the right-hand column and the bottom row all add up to the same number, which is always positive.

All Plus or Minus puzzles are copyright © Laird Stevens 2019.

50

PLUS OR MINUS Puzzle 51

4	6	1	2	9
6	4	2	5	1
5	1	4	3	5
5	2	6	2	5
8	7	3	2	

Put either a plus (+) or a minus (-) sign beside each number, so the numbers add up to the answers in the right-hand column and in the bottom row. The numbers in the diagonal, the right-hand column and the bottom row all add up to the same number, which is always positive.

PLUS OR MINUS Puzzle 52

9	4	2	3	6
4	6	5	4	9
4	5	6	3	4
1	7	2	3	1
8	8	5	1	

Put either a plus (+) or a minus (-) sign beside each number, so the numbers add up to the answers in the right-hand column and in the bottom row. The numbers in the diagonal, the right-hand column and the bottom row all add up to the same number, which is always positive.

PLUS OR MINUS

8	1	3	5	7
6	5	7	2	8
5	4	6	1	6
2	1	5	2	4
9	3	1	6	

Put either a plus (+) or a minus (-) sign beside each number, so the numbers add up to the answers in the right-hand column and in the bottom row. The numbers in the diagonal, the right-hand column and the bottom row all add up to the same number, which is always positive.

PLUS OR MINUS Puzzle 54

10	4	4	2	8
3	9	8	7	9
4	4	10	9	7
3	1	5	8	5
8	10	9	8	

Put either a plus (+) or a minus (-) sign beside each number, so the numbers add up to the answers in the right-hand column and in the bottom row. The numbers in the diagonal, the right-hand column and the bottom row all add up to the same number, which is always positive.

PLUS OR MINUS Puzzle 55

4	3	5	2	8
4	5	2	2	1
2	3	8	6	9
5	3	1	8	7
7	2	6	10	

Put either a plus (+) or a minus (-) sign beside each number, so the numbers add up to the answers in the right-hand column and in the bottom row. The numbers in the diagonal, the right-hand column and the bottom row all add up to the same number, which is always positive.

PLUS OR MINUS Puzzle 56

9	1	4	1	7
5	9	2	1	7
3	5	7	3	4
9	3	3	8	7
10	8	8	9	

Put either a plus (+) or a minus (-) sign beside each number, so the numbers add up to the answers in the right-hand column and in the bottom row. The numbers in the diagonal, the right-hand column and the bottom row all add up to the same number, which is always positive.

All Plus or Minus puzzles are copyright © Laird Stevens 2019.

PLUS OR MINUS Puzzle 57

5	6	3	5	9
8	7	4	2	7
7	1	9	8	7
1	6	9	4	2
7	4	7	7	

Put either a plus (+) or a minus (-) sign beside each number, so the numbers add up to the answers in the right-hand column and in the bottom row. The numbers in the diagonal, the right-hand column and the bottom row all add up to the same number, which is always positive.

All Plus or Minus puzzles are copyright © Laird Stevens 2019.

57

PLUS OR MINUS Puzzle 58

9	5	8	4	8
5	7	2	6	6
3	6	1	1	1
5	1	4	8	8
4	9	9	9	

Put either a plus (+) or a minus (-) sign beside each number, so the numbers add up to the answers in the right-hand column and in the bottom row. The numbers in the diagonal, the right-hand column and the bottom row all add up to the same number, which is always positive.

All Plus or Minus puzzles are copyright © Laird Stevens 2019.

58

PLUS OR MINUS

5	3	7	1	8
4	4	2	1	1
5	1	6	3	3
2	8	1	3	6
4	6	4	4	

Put either a plus (+) or a minus (-) sign beside each number, so the numbers add up to the answers in the right-hand column and in the bottom row. The numbers in the diagonal, the right-hand column and the bottom row all add up to the same number, which is always positive.

PLUS OR MINUS Puzzle 60

9	1	1	3	8
2	8	1	1	6
5	3	3	4	9
4	7	2	7	2
8	5	1	9	

Put either a plus (+) or a minus (-) sign beside each number, so the numbers add up to the answers in the right-hand column and in the bottom row. The numbers in the diagonal, the right-hand column and the bottom row all add up to the same number, which is always positive.

PLUS OR MINUS

+5	+7	+2	-4	+10
+6	+8	-2	-2	+10
+2	+1	+7	-2	+8
-4	-6	+2	+5	-3
+9	+10	+9	-3	**25**

Answer to Puzzle 1

PLUS OR MINUS

+5	+5	-3	-3	+4
-5	+8	-1	+2	+4
+1	-7	-2	+5	-3
+5	+3	-2	-7	-1
+6	+9	-8	-3	*4*

Answer to Puzzle 2

PLUS OR MINUS

+3	+1	+1	+3	+8
+2	+5	-8	-8	-9
+6	-5	+7	-1	+7
-2	+7	+4	-1	+8
+9	+8	+4	-7	*15*

Answer to Puzzle 3

PLUS OR MINUS

+8	+5	+3	-7	+9
+3	-7	+2	+9	+7
-7	+2	+5	-8	-8
+1	+4	-7	+4	+2
+5	+4	+3	-2	*10*

Answer to Puzzle 4

PLUS OR MINUS

+8	+2	+4	-5	+9
+5	-6	-4	-4	-9
+2	+2	-6	+8	+6
-6	-5	+1	+7	-3
+9	-7	-5	+6	*3*

Answer to Puzzle 5

PLUS OR MINUS

+5	-3	-1	+6	+7
-3	+6	-1	-7	-5
+3	-2	-5	+8	+4
+3	-5	+2	-4	-4
+8	-4	-5	+3	**2**

Answer to Puzzle 6

PLUS OR MINUS

+6	+5	-3	-1	+7
+6	-1	+2	+1	+8
-7	-2	+6	-2	-5
+3	-6	+4	+8	+9
+8	-4	+9	+6	*19*

Answer to Puzzle 7

PLUS OR MINUS

+6	-3	+2	+2	+7
+3	-2	+4	+2	+7
-7	-1	+3	-1	-6
-1	+3	-3	+6	+5
+1	-3	+6	+9	*13*

Answer to Puzzle 8

PLUS OR MINUS

+7	-9	-7	+4	-5
+5	+1	-6	-2	-2
+1	-9	+8	+9	+9
-4	+9	+9	-5	+9
+9	-8	+4	+6	*11*

Answer to Puzzle 9

PLUS OR MINUS

+10	+5	+4	-10	+9
-1	-5	+6	+6	+6
-9	+9	+7	-5	+2
+3	-1	-7	+7	+2
+3	+8	+10	-2	*19*

Answer to Puzzle 10

PLUS OR MINUS

+5	+5	-2	-4	+4
+2	+6	+4	-3	+9
+8	+2	-3	-3	+4
-9	-4	+4	+8	-1
+6	+9	+3	-2	*16*

Answer to Puzzle 11

PLUS OR MINUS

+7	-1	-2	+6	+10
+6	+9	-1	-6	+8
-2	-2	-2	+1	-5
-3	+3	+1	-2	-1
+8	+9	-4	-1	*12*

Answer to Puzzle 12

PLUS OR MINUS

+10	+5	-3	-2	+10
-1	+9	+8	-6	+10
+3	-1	-3	-3	-4
-2	-6	+8	+10	+10
+10	+7	+10	-1	*26*

Answer to Puzzle 13

PLUS OR MINUS

+8	-6	+4	+3	+9
+3	+7	+4	-5	+9
-3	+5	-9	+1	-6
-3	-1	-2	-2	-8
+5	+5	-3	-3	*4*

Answer to Puzzle 14

All Plus or Minus puzzles are copyright © Laird Stevens 2019.

PLUS OR MINUS

+9	+5	-2	-2	+10
-7	-4	+4	+1	-6
+8	-3	+8	-3	+10
-3	+5	-3	+8	+7
+7	+3	+7	+4	*21*

Answer to Puzzle 15

PLUS OR MINUS

+3	+2	+3	-1	+7
+8	-4	+5	-1	+8
+1	-4	+3	-5	-5
-3	-3	-2	-1	-9
+9	-9	+9	-8	*1*

Answer to Puzzle 16

PLUS OR MINUS

+7	-1	-3	+2	+5
-4	+8	+2	+3	+9
+1	-3	+7	+3	+8
+5	-2	-3	-4	-4
+9	+2	+3	+4	*18*

Answer to Puzzle 17

PLUS OR MINUS

+4	-5	+3	+3	+5
+1	+9	+3	-8	+5
+1	+1	-1	+4	+5
+1	-6	+2	+8	+5
+7	-1	+7	+7	*20*

Answer to Puzzle 18

PLUS OR MINUS

+4	+1	-4	+2	+3
-1	+6	+2	-2	+5
-5	-6	+8	-1	-4
+3	+8	+3	-7	+7
+1	+9	+9	-8	*11*

Answer to Puzzle 19

PLUS OR MINUS

+9	-4	-4	+1	+2
+6	-3	-2	+4	+5
-4	+5	-2	-2	-3
-4	-3	+7	-1	-1
+7	-5	-1	+2	*3*

Answer to Puzzle 20

PLUS OR MINUS

+3	+6	-4	-1	+4
-2	+7	+2	-3	+4
-1	-3	+9	-1	+4
+8	-2	+1	-2	+5
+8	+8	+8	-7	*17*

Answer to Puzzle 21

PLUS OR MINUS

+9	-1	+3	-1	+10
+5	+9	-4	-3	+7
-1	+5	+6	-1	+9
-3	-4	+5	+3	+1
+10	+9	+10	-2	**27**

Answer to Puzzle 22

PLUS OR MINUS

+8	+4	+4	-9	+7
-4	+7	+7	-2	+8
+8	+4	-9	+2	+5
-7	-9	+2	+7	-7
+5	+6	+4	-2	*13*

Answer to Puzzle 23

PLUS OR MINUS

+5	-3	+1	+2	+5
+3	-1	+2	-1	+3
-4	+2	+8	+3	+9
+3	-4	-4	+3	-2
+7	-6	+7	+7	*15*

Answer to Puzzle 24

PLUS OR MINUS

+8	-1	+3	-1	+9
+1	+8	-6	+1	+4
+1	-2	+8	+1	+8
-3	+4	+2	-4	-1
+7	+9	+7	-3	*20*

Answer to Puzzle 25

PLUS OR MINUS

+10	-2	+5	-4	+9
-1	+6	+2	-8	-1
+2	+7	-3	+1	+7
-3	-3	+4	+9	+7
+8	+8	+8	-2	**22**

Answer to Puzzle 26

PLUS OR MINUS

+9	+1	-3	+3	+10
-4	+9	+3	+1	+9
-4	-6	+9	-1	-2
+7	+4	-1	-2	+8
+8	+8	+8	+1	25

Answer to Puzzle 27

All Plus or Minus puzzles are copyright © Laird Stevens 2019.

PLUS OR MINUS

+7	+8	-4	-3	+8
+2	-1	-4	+2	-1
-2	-2	+10	+2	+8
+2	+4	-5	+8	+9
+9	+9	-3	+9	**24**

Answer to Puzzle 28

PLUS OR MINUS

+8	+3	-2	-2	+7
+6	-1	-3	+5	+7
-2	+6	+7	-4	+7
-3	+1	-5	+9	+2
+9	+9	-3	+8	**23**

Answer to Puzzle 29

PLUS OR MINUS

+3	+3	-5	+3	+4
-5	+4	+4	+3	+6
+3	+1	-5	-8	-9
+4	-2	-1	+7	+8
+5	+6	-7	+5	*9*

Answer to Puzzle 30

PLUS OR MINUS

+8	+6	+1	-8	+7
-4	+5	+3	+1	+5
-3	-4	+8	+7	+8
+5	+2	-6	+7	+8
+6	+9	+6	+7	*28*

Answer to Puzzle 31

PLUS OR MINUS

+7	+3	-2	-3	+5
-3	-8	+3	+7	-1
-6	+1	+6	-2	-1
+7	-2	-3	-3	-1
+5	-6	+4	-1	**2**

Answer to Puzzle 32

PLUS OR MINUS

+6	-2	+1	-1	+4
-2	+7	+5	-5	+5
+3	+3	-4	+3	+5
-4	-4	+3	-4	-9
+3	+4	+5	-7	*5*

Answer to Puzzle 33

PLUS OR MINUS

+7	-2	-2	-2	+1
-4	+5	-3	+5	+3
+5	+5	-3	-2	+5
-3	-3	+6	-3	-3
+5	+5	-2	-2	*6*

Answer to Puzzle 34

PLUS OR MINUS

+2	+2	+5	-4	+5
+5	+2	-3	+1	+5
-2	-1	+2	-5	-6
+1	+2	-1	+1	+3
+6	+5	+3	-7	**7**

Answer to Puzzle 35

PLUS OR MINUS

+4	+1	+1	-4	+2
-8	+4	+3	+3	+2
+3	-2	-4	-1	-4
+3	-1	+2	+4	+8
+2	+2	+2	+2	*8*

Answer to Puzzle 36

PLUS OR MINUS

+2	+3	-4	+3	+4
-3	+7	-1	-6	-3
-1	-3	+8	+2	+6
+8	-1	+3	-5	+5
+6	+6	+6	-6	*12*

Answer to Puzzle 37

PLUS OR MINUS

+4	+8	+7	-2	+17
+5	+5	+5	-7	+8
-3	-4	-3	+4	-6
+2	-7	-8	+9	-4
+8	+2	+1	+4	*15*

Answer to Puzzle 38

PLUS OR MINUS

+9	-7	+4	+1	+7
-2	+8	-6	-1	-1
-4	+2	+7	+3	+8
+5	+2	+3	-6	+4
+8	+5	+8	-3	*18*

Answer to Puzzle 39

PLUS OR MINUS

+6	+2	+1	-4	+5
-2	+6	-1	+2	+5
-1	+1	-3	+1	-2
+4	-2	-1	+7	+8
+7	+7	-4	+6	*16*

Answer to Puzzle 40

PLUS OR MINUS

+5	-3	-4	-2	-4
+5	+6	-1	-4	+6
-6	+2	+7	+4	+7
+4	+3	+2	-1	+8
+8	+8	+4	-3	*17*

Answer to Puzzle 41

PLUS OR MINUS

+10	+5	-7	+1	+9
+4	+10	-1	-4	+9
-9	+3	+10	+5	+9
+5	-10	+8	-1	+2
+10	+8	+10	+1	**29**

Answer to Puzzle 42

PLUS OR MINUS

+8	+3	-6	+2	+7
-3	+6	-5	+1	-1
+1	-4	-4	+5	-2
-2	+2	+6	-9	-3
+4	+7	-9	-1	*1*

Answer to Puzzle 43

PLUS OR MINUS

+8	-6	+9	-1	+10
-6	+9	+1	-5	-1
+5	-1	-2	+4	+6
-2	+5	-3	+9	+9
+5	+7	+5	+7	**24**

Answer to Puzzle 44

PLUS OR MINUS

+4	+2	+4	-3	+7
+4	+6	+1	-7	+4
+3	+4	-9	+1	-1
-6	-5	+2	+8	-1
+5	+7	-2	-1	*9*

Answer to Puzzle 45

PLUS OR MINUS

+6	+5	+4	-6	+9
-7	+8	+6	+2	+9
+3	-3	+5	-1	+4
+6	-2	-7	+4	+1
+8	+8	+8	-1	**23**

Answer to Puzzle 46

PLUS OR MINUS

+7	+4	-5	+3	+9
-5	+8	-3	+4	+4
+1	-3	+2	+1	+1
+5	-3	+1	-9	-6
+8	+6	-5	-1	*8*

Answer to Puzzle 47

PLUS OR MINUS

+8	+7	-1	-4	+10
-3	+5	+5	+2	+9
+7	-4	+8	-2	+9
-4	+1	-4	+1	-6
+8	+9	+8	-3	**22**

Answer tp Puzzle 48

PLUS OR MINUS

+9	+4	-10	+5	+8
+3	+4	+3	-1	+9
+2	-5	+2	-3	-4
-4	+3	+3	-8	-6
+10	+6	-2	-7	**7**

Answer to Puzzle 49

PLUS OR MINUS

+7	+4	-6	+5	+10
+5	+4	+8	-9	+8
-1	+7	+4	-5	+5
-3	-6	+1	+4	-4
+8	+9	+7	-5	*19*

Answer to Puzzle 50

PLUS OR MINUS

+4	+6	+1	-2	+9
-6	+4	-2	+5	+1
+5	-1	+4	-3	+5
+5	-2	-6	-2	-5
+8	+7	-3	-2	*10*

Answer to Puzzle 51

PLUS OR MINUS

-9	+4	+2	-3	-6
+4	+6	-5	+4	+9
-4	+5	+6	-3	+4
+1	-7	+2	+3	-1
-8	+8	+5	+1	*6*

Answer to Puzzle 52

PLUS OR MINUS

+8	+1	+3	-5	+7
-6	+5	+7	+2	+8
+5	-4	-6	-1	-6
+2	+1	-5	-2	-4
+9	+3	-1	-6	*5*

Answer to Puzzle 53

PLUS OR MINUS

+10	-4	+4	-2	+8
-3	+9	-8	-7	-9
+4	+4	-10	+9	+7
-3	+1	+5	-8	-5
+8	+10	-9	-8	*1*

Answer to Puzzle 54

PLUS OR MINUS

-4	+3	-5	-2	-8
+4	-5	+2	-2	-1
-2	-3	+8	+6	+9
-5	+3	+1	+8	+7
-7	-2	+6	+10	**7**

Answer to Puzzle 55

PLUS OR MINUS

+9	+1	-4	+1	+7
-5	+9	+2	+1	+7
-3	-5	+7	-3	-4
+9	+3	+3	-8	+7
+10	+8	+8	-9	*17*

Answer to Puzzle 56

PLUS OR MINUS

+5	+6	+3	-5	+9
+8	-7	+4	+2	+7
-7	-1	+9	-8	-7
+1	+6	-9	+4	+2
+7	+4	+7	-7	*11*

Answer to Puzzle 57

PLUS OR MINUS

+9	-5	+8	-4	+8
-5	+7	-2	+6	+6
-3	+6	-1	-1	+1
-5	+1	+4	+8	+8
-4	+9	+9	+9	**23**

Answer to Puzzle 58

PLUS OR MINUS

+5	-3	+7	-1	+8
-4	+4	+2	-1	+1
+5	+1	-6	+3	+3
-2	-8	+1	+3	-6
+4	-6	+4	+4	*6*

Answer to Puzzle 59

PLUS OR MINUS

+9	+1	+1	-3	+8
-2	+8	-1	+1	+6
+5	+3	-3	+4	+9
-4	-7	+2	+7	-2
+8	+5	-1	+9	*21*

Answer to Puzzle 60